MOST POPULAR
COCKTAILS
MODERN AND CLASSIC MIXED DRINKS

IAN BIRELL

COPYRIGHT © IAN BIRELL, 2019
ALL RIGHTS RESERVED

No part of this publication or the information in it may be quoted from or reproduced in any form by means such as printing, scanning, photocopying or otherwise without prior written permission of the copyright holder.

ISBN 978-1-09-919028-5

Contents

Introduction 7
Cocktail Making Techniques 9
Glassware 11
Gadgets 13

RUM BASED COCKTAILS 15
   Apple Cooler 17
   Beachcomber 18
   Blue Hawaiian 19
   Cable Car.. 20
   Cuba Libre 21
   Daiquiri 22
   Dark'n'Stormy... 23
   Hurricane 24
   Knickerbocker.. 26
   Mai Tai 27
   Mojito 29
   Painkiller 31
   Piña Colada 33
   Planter's Punch.. 34
   Rum Runner 36

GIN BASED COCKTAILS 37
   Aviation 39
   Clover Club... 40
   Bramble.. 41
   Bronx 43
   Dry Martini 44
   Gimlet... 45
   Gin and Tonic 46
   Martinez 47
   Negroni 48
   Tom Collins..49

Vesper 51

VODKA BASED COCKTAILS 53
   Black Russian.. 55
   Blue Lagoon.. 56
   Bloody Mary.. 57
   Caipiroska 59
   Cape Codder 60
   Cosmopolitan.. 61
   Espresso Martini... 63
   IQ 64
   Kamikadze 65
   Long Island Iced Tea 66
   Moscow Mule 68
   Oldboy... 69
   Salty Dog 71
   Sea Breeze 72
   Sex on the Beach 73
   Screwdriver... 75
   Vodka Martini.. 76
   White Russian 77

TEQUILA BASED COCKTAILS 79
   Duke Tulip... 81
   Kerman.. 83
   Margarita... 84
   Monte Alban 85
   Old George 87
   Paloma.. 89
   Primavera 91
   Tequila Smash 93
   Tequila Sunrise... 94

BRANDY BASED COCKTAILS 95
   Brandy Alexander 97

Brandy Sour 98
French Cinnamon 100
French Connection 101
Horse's Neck 102
Ruby 103
The Double 104
Sidecar 105
Sunset Boulevard 106

WHISKY BASED COCKTAILS 107
Boulevardier 109
Manhattan 110
Match Point 111
Mint Julep 112
Old Fashioned 113
Rob Roy 114
Rusty Nail 115
The New Yorker 116
Whiskey Sour 117

INDEX 119

Introduction

"I drink to make other people more interesting."
– Ernest Hemingway

Some of the best cocktails were created over a century ago. These are the timeless favorites that have tantalized and whetted the palates of generations of drinkers.

Sure, the modern cocktail scene is filled with many great drinks that will astound and amaze the most refined palates. Yet, these classic cocktails have stood up to the tests of time, survived Prohibition, and witnessed amazing changes in the booze that is poured into them. We keep going back to them, and for very good reasons: they are simply great drinks.

Unless you're still an undergrad, it's time to move on from making rum and Cokes or vodka sodas at the bar. After all, you're a grown-up, and you should be drinking grown-up drinks. In this book you will find recipes of most popular bar drinks that you can make.

Follow the recipes in this book, then experiment and tweak them to your own liking. Drinks are not a one-size-fits-all experience and these are simply a foundation that you can use to build a true appreciation for everything the cocktail world has to offer.

Cocktail Making Techniques

Here are some techniques you need to know to make cocktails from this book.

Blending is an appropriate way of combining ingredients, creating a smooth ready to serve mixture. Some recipes will call for ice to be placed in the blender, in which case you would use a suitable amount of crushed ice. An electric blender is needed for recipes containing ingredients which do not break down by shaking.

When **building** a cocktail, the ingredients are poured into the glass in which the cocktail will be served. Usually, the ingredients are floated on top of each other, but occasionally, a swizzle stick is put in the glass, allowing the ingredients to be mixed.

Shaking is the method by which you use a cocktail shaker to mix ingredients together and chill them simultaneously. The object is to almost freeze the drink whilst breaking down and combining the ingredients. Normally this is done with ice cubes three-quarters of the way full. When you've poured in the ingredients, hold the shaker in both hands, with one hand on top and one supporting the base, and give a short, sharp, snappy shake. It's important not to rock your cocktail to sleep. When water has begun to condense on the surface of the shaker, the cocktail should be sufficiently chilled and ready to be strained.

You can **stir** cocktails effectively with a metal or glass rod in a mixing glass. If ice is to be used, use ice cubes to prevent dilution, and strain the contents into a glass when the surface of the mixing glass begins to collect condensation.

Glassware

If you've ever tried to stock a bar cart or set up a home bar, you've probably been confused by all of the different types of cocktail glasses. You will need these ten types of cocktail glasses to make cocktails from this book.

Champagne saucer

Cocktail glass

Goblet glass

Highball/Collins glass

Hurricane glass

Margarita glass

Rocks glass

Sling glass

Sour glass

Champagne saucer. A glass with a tall stem and wide bowl. According to legend, it was designed to resemble the silhouette of one of the King of France's mistresses. Used to serve champagne and tiki cocktails. Standard capacity: 7-10 oz.

Cocktail glass. Also known as a martini glass, this was one of the first glasses in which cocktails were served without ice. Before serving, the glass must be chilled, and the long stem prevents the cocktail from warming up in the hand. Standard capacity: 3-5 oz.

Goblet glass. A royal glass with thick walls, permitting the clinking of glasses while drinking without the risk of breaking. Standard capacity: 6-10 oz.

Highball glass. A tall glass for water, juice or club mixes. Mixes are built right in the glass. Standard capacity: 10-13 oz.

Collins glass. A tall glass for long and mixed drinks. Named after the classic "Tom Collins" cocktail. Standard capacity: 10-13 oz.

Hurricane glass. An old-fashioned glass resembling a kerosene lamp, used for serving tropical drinks, named in honor of Pat O'Brien's cocktail of the same name. Standard capacity: 10-15 oz.

Margarita glass. In a past life, it was a simple container for guacamole, but now it is the signature glass for serving the most famous tequila-based cocktail in the world. Standard capacity: 8-12 oz.

Rocks glass. A Wide glass with a thick bottom, used to serve strong spirits or cocktails in a pure, undiluted form. Standard capacity: 6-10 oz.

Sling glass. The quintessential glass for serving the eponymous cocktail, which would become the calling card of the Raffles Hotel. Standard capacity: 7-10 oz.

Sour glass. Designed to hold Sour cocktails, which contain a base liquor, lemon or lime juice, and a sweetener. Standard capacity: 3-4 oz.

Gadgets

Bar spoon. This indispensable bartender's tool is used for preparing cocktails in a mixing glass and for making layers in shots, as well as to measure ⅛ oz. portions of liquids or dry ingredients

Blender. Invented in 1922 by Stephen Poplawski, this electric appliance is indispensable for making tiki cocktails, smoothies and froz.en drinks

Clothespins. A decorative accessory used to hold garnishes to the glass

Cocktail skewer. A decorative accessory for serving olives in martinis and cocktail cherries in Manhattans. First appeared in bars at the end of the 19th century, thanks to the marketing genius Charles Forster

Drinking straws. In 1888, Marvin Stone, the owner of a paper mouthpiece factory, invented the best accessory for drinking drinks from glasses. Joseph Friedman then made a fortune by developing flexible drinking straws. The final step was to make straws from plastic

Jigger. Ensures accurate and ideal portions in cocktails. The best bartenders always have a range of sizes in their arsenal: ½-1 oz., ¼-¾ oz. and 1-2 oz.

Mixing glass. Used to prepare strong, masculine drinks without added juices, herbs or jams. Ice keeps its form and does not melt, maintaining the drink's strength. Standard capacity 16-30 oz..

Muddler. An indispensable accessory for tropical cocktails, this crushes berries and fruits either in the shaker or directly in the glass

Nutmeg grater. A useful accessory for preparing nutmeg or chocolate powder, or even zest from citrus fruits

Shaker. It took its current form at the end of the 1800s, and earned especial popularity in the 1920s and 1930s through doz.ens of different styles and forms. They are divided into categories: cobbler shakers, which have a built-in strainer; French shakers, without a strainer; and Boston shakers, which consist of two equal-sized cups. Standard capacity 15-25 oz.

Sieve. Used together with shakers and strainers for double filtration of cocktails when pouring them from the shaker into the glass. With a finer net than a strainer, it does not allow even the smallest fruit seeds and bits of ice to fall into the drink

Strainer. An accessory indispensable when working with Boston or French shakers. Used for filtering fruit pits, pieces of ice and other undesired ingredients out of drinks

Squeezer. An indispensable tool for squeezing juice from limes and lemons. Despite the fact that most popular establishments nowadays use pre-prepared juice, freshly-squeezed juice is a mark of higher quality

Zest knife. A bartending tool sourced from the Japanese culture of carving. Used to cut off thin layers of zest, or make rings or twists from apples

RUM BASED COCKTAILS

Apple Cooler

prep time: 5 min | technique: build

Ingredients:
2 oz. white rum
4 oz. apple juice
2 oz. Sprite
Ice
Apple, for garnish

Gadgets:
highball glass, jigger, bar spoon, drinking straws

Preparation:
. Fill a highball glass to the top with ice
. Pour in 3 ½ oz. of apple juice and 1 ½ oz. of white rum
. Top up with Sprite and stir gently
. Garnish with 3 apple wedges

Beachcomber

prep time: 3 min | technique: shake

Ingredients:
2 oz. white rum
¾ oz. triple sec liqueur
¼ oz. Maraschino liqueur
¾ oz. lime juice
Ice
Lime wedge, for garnish

Gadgets:
cocktail glass, squeezer, jigger, shaker, strainer

Preparation:
. Pour ¾ oz. of lime juice, ¾ oz. of triple sec liqueur, ¼ oz. of Maraschino liqueur and 2 oz. of white rum into a shaker
. Fill the shaker with ice cubes and shake
. Strain into a chilled cocktail glass
. Garnish with a lime wedge

Blue Hawaiian

prep time: 5 min | technique: build

Ingredients:
1½ oz. white rum
1 oz. blue curacao liqueur
1 oz. creme de coconut
2 oz. pineapple juice
Ice
Maraschino cherry, for garnish
Pineapple, for garnish

Gadgets:
hurricane glass, mixing glass, bar spoon, strainer, jigger, cocktail skewer

Preparation:
. Pour 1 oz. of blue curacao liqueur, 1 oz. of creme de coconut, 2 oz. of pineapple juice and 1½ oz. of white rum into a mixing glass
. Fill the glass with ice cubes and stir gently
. Strain into a chilled hurricane glass
. Garnish with a Maraschino cherry and a pineapple wedge

Cable Car

prep time: 5 min | technique: shake

Ingredients:
1½ oz. spiced rum
1 oz. orange curacao liqueur
1 oz. lemon juice
½ oz. sugar syrup
Ice
Orange peel spiral, for garnish
Superfine sugar, for rimming

Gadgets:
cocktail glass, shaker, strainer, jigger,

Preparation:
. Rim a chilled cocktail glass with sugar
. Pour 1 oz. of lemon juice, ½ oz. of sugar syrup, 1 oz. of orange curacao liqueur and 1½ oz. spiced rum into a shaker
. Fill the shaker with ice cubes and shake
. Strain into prepared glass
. Garnish with orange peel spiral

Cuba Libre

prep time: 5 min | technique: build

Ingredients:
2 oz. gold rum
½ oz. lime juice
5 oz. cola
Ice
Lime, for garnish

Gadgets:
highball glass, jigger, squeezer, bar spoon, drinking straws

Preparation:
. Fill a highball glass to the top with ice
. Pour in ½ oz. of lime juice and 2 oz. of gold rum
. Top up with cola and stir gently
. Garnish with 2 lime wheels

Daiquiri

prep time: 3 min | technique: shake

Ingredients:
2 oz. white rum
½ oz. sugar syrup
1 oz. lime juice
Ice

Gadgets:
champagne saucer, squeezer, jigger, shaker, strainer

Preparation:
. Pour 1 of lime juice, ½ oz. of sugar syrup and 2 oz. of white rum into a shaker
. Fill the shaker with ice cubes and shake
. Strain into a chilled champagne saucer

Dark'n'Stormy

prep time: 5 min | technique: build

Ingredients:
2 oz. black rum
3 oz. ginger beer
½ oz. lime juice
Ice
Lime, for garnish

Gadgets:
highball glass, jigger, squeezer, bar spoon, drinking straws

Preparation:
. Fill a highball glass to the top with ice
. Pour in ½ oz. of lime juice, 3 oz. of ginger beer and 2 oz. of black rum
. Stir gently
. Garnish with a lime wedge

Hurricane

prep time: 5 min | technique: shake

Ingredients:
2 oz. light rum
2 oz. dark rum
2 oz. passion fruit juice
1 oz. orange juice
1 oz. lime juice
½ oz. sugar syrup
½ oz. grenadine
Maraschino cherry
Orange slice
Ice

Gadgets:
hurricane glass, squeezer, jigger, shaker, strainer, drinking straws

Preparation:
. Pour 2 oz. of passion fruit juice, 1 oz. of orange juice, 1 oz. of lime juice, ½ oz. of sugar syrup, ½

oz. of grenadine, 2 oz. of light rum and 2 oz. of dark rum into a shaker
. Fill the shaker with ice cubes and shake
. Strain into a chilled hurricane glass
. Garnish with a Maraschino cherry and orange wheel

Knickerbocker

prep time: 3 min | technique: shake

Ingredients:
1½ oz. white rum
¾ oz. dry orange liqueur
½ oz. raspberry syrup
½ oz. lime juice
Ice

Gadgets:
cocktail glass, squeezer, jigger, shaker, strainer

Preparation:
. Pour ½ oz. of lime juice, ½ oz. of raspberry syrup, ¾ oz. of dry orange liqueur and 1½ oz. of white rum into a shaker
. Fill the shaker with ice cubes and shake
. Strain into a chilled cocktail glass

Mai Tai

prep time: 5 min | technique: shake

Ingredients:
2 oz. aged rum
¾ oz. dry orange liqueur
½ oz. sugar syrup
½ oz. almond syrup
¾ oz. lime juice
Pineapple
Mint
Red maraschino cherry
Crushed ice
Ice cubes

Gadgets:
rocks glass, squeezer, jigger, shaker, strainer, drinking straws

Preparation:
. Fill a rocks glass to the top with crushed ice

. Pour ¾ oz. of lime juice, ½ oz. of sugar syrup, ½ oz. of almond syrup, ¾ oz. of dry orange liqueur and 2 oz. of aged rum into a shaker
. Fill the shaker with ice cubes and shake
. Strain into the rocks glass
. Top up with crushed ice
. Garnish with a Maraschino cherry, a pineapple wedge and a mint sprig

Mojito

prep time: 5 min | technique: build

Ingredients:
2 oz. white rum
½ oz. sugar syrup
3 oz. club soda
Lime
Mint
Crushed ice

Gadgets:
highball glass, muddler, jigger, bar spoon, drinking straws

Preparation:
. Place 3 lime wedges into a highball glass and muddle
. Take 10 mint leaves and "clap" them between your hands
. Place the mint into the highball glass

- Fill the highball glass to the top with crushed ice
- Add ½ oz. of sugar syrup and 2 oz. of white rum
- Top up with club soda and stir gently
- Top up with crushed ice
- Garnish with a mint sprig

Painkiller

prep time: 5 min | technique: shake

Ingredients:
2 oz. dark rum
4 oz. pineapple juice
1 oz. orange juice
1 oz. coconut cream
Nutmeg
Maraschino cherry
Orange slice
Ice

Gadgets:
highball glass, jigger, shaker, strainer, drinking straws, cocktail skewer

Preparation:
. Fill a highball glass to the top with ice
. Pour 4 oz. of pineapple juice, 1 oz. of orange juice, 1 oz. of coconut cream and 2 oz. of dark rum into a shaker

- Fill the shaker with ice cubes and shake
- Strain into a chilled highball glass
- Sprinkle grated nutmeg on top
- Garnish with an orange slice and a Maraschino cherry on a cocktail skewer

Piña Colada

prep time: 6 min | technique: blend

Ingredients:
1 oz. white rum
1 oz. coconut cream
3 oz. pineapple juice
Ice
Maraschino cherry
Pineapple wedge

Gadgets:
hurricane glass, blender, bar spoon, squeezer, jigger, scoop, cocktail umbrella, drinking straws

Preparation:
. Place 6 bar spoons of coconut cream into a blender
. Pour in 3 oz. of pineapple juice and 1 oz. of white rum
. Add a scoop of crushed ice and blend
. Pour into a hurricane glass
. Garnish with a pineapple wedge, a Maraschino cherry and a cocktail umbrella

Planter's Punch

prep time: 5 min | technique: shake

Ingredients:
1½ oz. dark rum
1 oz. orange juice
1 oz. pineapple juice
¾ oz. lemon juice
½ oz. grenadine syrup
¼ oz. sugar syrup
1 dash Angostura bitters
Ice
Maraschino cherry
Orange wheel
Pineapple wedge

Gadgets:
highball glass, squeezer, jigger, shaker, strainer

Preparation:
. Fill a highball glass to the top with ice

- Pour 1 oz. of pineapple juice, 1 oz. of orange juice, ¾ oz. of lemon juice
- Add ¼ oz. of sugar syrup, ½ oz. of grenadine syrup, 1 dash of Angostura bitters and 1½ oz. dark rum
- Fill the shaker with ice cubes and shake
- Strain into the highball glass
- Sprinkle grated nutmeg on top
- Garnish with an orange wheel, a pineapple wedge and a red Maraschino cherry

Rum Runner

prep time: 5 min | technique: shake

Ingredients:
1 oz. light rum
1 oz. dark rum
1 oz. pineapple juice
1 oz. orange juice
1 oz. blackberry liqueur
1 oz. banana liqueur
½ oz. grenadine
Orange wheel, for garnish

Gadgets:
rocks glass, squeezer, jigger, shaker, strainer

Preparation:
. Pour 1 oz. of pineapple juice, 1 oz. of orange juice, 1 oz. of blackberry liqueur, 1 oz. of banana liqueur, ½ oz. of grenadine, 1 oz. of white rum and 1 oz. of dark rum into a shaker
. Fill the shaker with ice cubes and shake
. Strain into a chilled rocks glass
. Garnish with an orange wheel

GIN BASED COCKTAILS

Aviation

prep time: 5 min | technique: stir

Ingredients:
1½ oz. gin
¾ oz. Maraschino liqueur
¼ oz. violet liqueur
½ oz. lemon juice
Ice
Lemon zest, for garnish

Gadgets:
cocktail glass, mixing glass, squeezer, bar spoon, strainer, jigger

Preparation:
. Pour ½ oz. of lemon juice, ¾ oz. of Maraschino liqueur, ¼ oz. of violet liqueur and 1½ oz. of gin into a mixing glass
. Fill the glass with ice cubes and stir gently
. Strain into a chilled cocktail glass
. Garnish with lemon zest

Clover Club

prep time: 5 min | technique: shake

Ingredients:
1 ½ oz. gin
1 oz. raspberry syrup
½ oz. lime juice
1 egg white
Ice
Mint leaf, for garnish

Gadgets:
cocktail glass, squeezer, jigger, shaker, strainer

Preparation:
. Pour 1 egg white, ½ oz. of lime juice, 1 oz. of raspberry syrup and 2 oz. of gin into a shaker
. Fill the shaker with ice cubes and shake thoroughly
. Strain into a chilled cocktail glass
. Garnish with a mint leaf

Bramble

prep time: 5 min | technique: build

Ingredients:
1½ oz. gin
½ oz. Pedro Ximenez sherry
½ oz. sugar syrup
¾ oz. lime juice
Balsamic vinegar
Raspberry
Caster sugar
Crushed ice

Gadgets:
rocks glass, muddler, teaspoon, squeezer, jigger, bar spoon, drinking straws

Preparation:
. Place 4 raspberries into rocks glass and muddle
. Fill the glass to the top with crushed ice

. Pour in ¾ oz. of lemon juice, ½ oz. of sugar syrup, ½ oz. of Pedro Ximenez sherry and 1½ oz. of gin
. Add 2 dashes of balsamic vinegar and stir gently
. Top up with crushed ice
. Garnish with a teaspoon and a raspberry, sprinkled with caster sugar

Bronx

prep time: 3 min | technique: shake

Ingredients:
1 oz. gin
½ oz. red vermouth
½ oz. dry vermouth
¾ oz. orange juice
Ice

Gadgets:
cocktail glass, jigger, shaker, strainer

Preparation:
. Pour ¾ oz. of orange juice, ½ oz. of red vermouth, ½ oz. of dry vermouth and 1 oz. of gin into a shaker
. Fill the shaker with ice cubes and shake
. Strain into a chilled cocktail glass

Dry Martini

prep time: 3 min | technique: stir

Ingredients:
2 ½ oz. gin
½ oz. dry vermouth Martini
Ice
Green olives, for garnish

Gadgets:
cocktail glass, mixing glass, bar spoon, strainer, jigger, cocktail skewer

Preparation:
. Pour ½ oz. of dry vermouth and 2 ½ oz. of gin into a mixing glass
. Fill the glass with ice cubes and stir gently
. Strain into a chilled cocktail glass
. Garnish with green olive on a cocktail skewer

Gimlet

prep time: 3 min | technique: shake

Ingredients:
2 oz. gin
1 oz. lime juice
Ice
Lime zest, for garnish

Gadgets:
cocktail glass, squeezer, jigger, shaker, strainer

Preparation:
. Pour 1 oz. of lime juice and 2 oz. of gin into a shaker
. Fill the shaker with ice cubes and shake
. Strain into a chilled cocktail glass
. Garnish with lime zest

Gin and Tonic

prep time: 5 min | technique: build

Ingredients:
1½ oz. gin
5 oz. tonic
Ice
Lime, for garnish

Gadgets:
highball glass, jigger, bar spoon, drinking straws

Preparation:
. Fill a highball glass to the top with ice
. Pour in 1½ oz. of gin
. Top up with tonic and stir gently
. Garnish with 2 lime wheels

Martinez

prep time: 3 min | technique: stir

Ingredients:
2 oz. gin
1 oz. red vermouth
¼ oz. Maraschino liqueur
Orange bitters
Orange zest
Ice

Gadgets:
cocktail glass, mixing glass, bar spoon, strainer, jigger

Preparation:
. Pour ¼ oz. of Maraschino liqueur, 1 oz. of red vermouth and 2 oz. of gin into a mixing glass
. Add 1 dash of orange bitters
. Fill the glass with ice cubes and stir gently
. Strain into a chilled cocktail glass
. Squeeze orange zest over the glass and put into the cocktail

Negroni

prep time: 3 min | technique: build

Ingredients:
1 oz. gin
1 oz. red vermouth
1 oz. red bitter
Ice
Orange, for garnish

Gadgets:
rocks glass, jigger, bar spoon

Preparation:
. Fill a rocks glass to the top with ice
. Pour in 1 oz. of red vermouth, 1 oz. of red bitter and 1 oz. of gin
. Stir gently
. Garnish with an orange wheel

Tom Collins

prep time: 5 min | technique: shake

Ingredients:
1½ oz. gin
¾ oz. sugar syrup
¾ oz. lemon juice
3½ oz. club soda
Ice
Orange, for garnish
Maraschino cherry, for garnish

Gadgets:
collins glass, squeezer, jigger, shaker, strainer, bar spoon, drinking straws

Preparation:
. Fill a collins glass to the top with ice cubes
. Pour ¾ oz. of lemon juice, ¾ oz. of sugar syrup and 1½ oz. of gin into a shaker
. Fill the shaker with ice cubes and shake

. Strain into the collins glass
. Top up with club soda and stir gently
. Garnish with an orange wheel and a red Maraschino cherry

Vesper

prep time: 3 min | technique: stir

Ingredients:
1½ oz. gin
½ oz. vodka
¼ oz. lillet blanc
Ice
Lemon zest, for garnish

Gadgets:
cocktail glass, mixing glass, bar spoon, strainer, jigger

Preparation:
. Pour ¼ oz. of lillet blanc, ½ oz. of vodka and 1½ oz. of gin into a mixing glass
. Fill the mixing glass with ice cubes and stir gently
. Strain into a chilled cocktail glass
. Rub lemon zest over the rim of the glass and garnish the cocktail with it

VODKA BASED COCKTAILS

Black Russian

prep time: 3 min | technique: build

Ingredients:
2 oz. vodka
1 oz. coffee liqueur
Ice

Gadgets:
rocks glass, jigger, bar spoon, drinking straws

Preparation:
. Fill a rocks glass to the top with ice
. Pour in 1 oz. of coffee liqueur and 2 oz. of vodka
. Stir gently

Blue Lagoon

prep time: 5 min | technique: build

Ingredients:
2 oz. vodka
1 oz. blue curacao liqueur
5 oz. lemonade
Ice
Pineapple, for garnish

Gadgets:
hurricane glass, jigger, bar spoon, drinking straws

Preparation:
. Fill a hurricane glass to the top with ice
. Pour in 1 oz. of blue curacao liqueur and 2 oz. of vodka
. Top up with lemonade and stir gently
. Garnish with a pineapple wedge

Bloody Mary

prep time: 5 min | technique: shake

Ingredients:
1½ oz. vodka
3 oz. tomato juice
½ oz. lemon juice
Worcestershire Sauce
Tabasco
Celery salt
Ground Black Pepper
Ice
Celery, for garnish

Gadgets:
highball glass, shaker, strainer, jigger, squeezer, drinking straws

Preparation:
. Fill a highball glass to the top with ice

- Pour ½ oz. of lemon juice, 3 oz. of tomato juice into a shaker
- Pour 1 ½ oz. of vodka into a shaker
- Add 3 dashes of Tabasco and 2 dashes of Worcestershire sauce
- Add a pinch of celery salt and a pinch of ground black pepper
- Fill the shaker with ice, close it and roll vertically from one hand to another for a few minutes
- Strain into the highball glass and garnish with a celery stalk

Caipiroska

prep time: 3 min | technique: build

Ingredients:
2 oz. vodka
¾ oz. sugar syrup
Ice
Lime

Gadgets:
rocks glass, jigger, bar spoon, muddler, drinking straws

Preparation:
. Place 2 lime wedges into a rocks glass and muddle
. Fill a rocks glass to the top with ice
. Pour in ¾ oz. of sugar syrup and 2 oz. of vodka
. Stir gently
. Top up with crushed ice
. Garnish with a lime wedge

Cape Codder

prep time: 5 min | technique: build

Ingredients:
2 oz. vodka
5 oz. cranberry juice
Ice
Cranberry, for garnish
Lime wedge, for garnish

Gadgets:
highball glass, jigger, bar spoon, drinking straws

Preparation:
. Fill a highball glass to the top with ice
. Pour in 2 oz. of vodka
. Top up with cranberry juice and stir gently
. Garnish with a lime wedge and cranberries

Cosmopolitan

prep time: 5 min | technique: shake

Ingredients:
1½ oz. vodka
¾ oz. triple sec liqueur
2 oz. cranberry juice
¼ oz. lime juice
Orange zest
Ice

Gadgets:
cocktail glass, shaker, strainer, jigger, squeezer, zest knife, culinary torch

Preparation:
. Pour ¼ oz. of lime juice, 2 oz. of cranberry juice ¾ oz. of triple sec liqueur and 1½ oz. of vodka into a shaker
. Fill the shaker with ice cubes and shake
. Strain into a chilled cocktail glass

. Use a culinary torch to flambée the oils from the orange zest over the cocktail
. Rim the sides of the glass with flamed orange zest and put it in the glass

Espresso Martini

prep time: 5 min | technique: shake

Ingredients:
1 oz. vodka
1 oz. coffee liqueur
1½ oz. espresso coffee
¼ oz. vanilla syrup
Ice
Coffee beans, for garnish

Gadgets:
cocktail glass, shaker, strainer, jigger, coffee machine

Preparation:
. Pour 1½ oz. of chilled espresso, ¼ oz. of vanilla syrup, 1 oz. of coffee liqueur and 1 oz. of vodka into a shaker
. Fill the shaker with ice cubes and shake
. Strain into a chilled cocktail glass
. Garnish with coffee beans

IQ

prep time: 5 min | technique: build

Ingredients:
2 oz. vodka
½ oz. honey syrup
5 oz. grapefruit juice
Ice
Orange zest, for garnish

Gadgets:
highball glass, jigger, bar spoon, drinking straws, cocktail skewer

Preparation:
. Fill a highball glass to the top with ice
. Pour in ½ oz. of honey syrup and 2 oz. of vodka
. Top up with grapefruit juice and stir gently
. Garnish with orange zest

Kamikadze

prep time: 5 min | technique: shake

Ingredients:
1½ oz. vodka
1 oz. triple sec liqueur
1 oz. lime juice
Ice
Lime wedge, for garnish

Gadgets:
cocktail glass, squeezer, jigger, shaker, strainer

Preparation:
. Pour 1 oz. of lime juice, 1 oz. of triple sec liqueur and 1½ oz. of vodka into a shaker
. Fill the shaker with ice cubes and shake
. Strain into a chilled cocktail glass
. Garnish with a lime wedge

Long Island Iced Tea

prep time: 6 min | technique: build

Ingredients:
½ oz. vodka
½ oz. white rum
½ oz. gin
½ oz. tequila
½ oz. triple sec liqueur
½ oz. sugar syrup
½ oz. lemon juice
4 oz. cola
Lime wedge, for garnish

Gadgets:
highball glass, jigger, bar spoon, drinking straws

Preparation:
. Fill a highball glass to the top with ice
. Pour in ½ oz. of sugar syrup, ½ oz. of lemon juice, ½ oz. of triple sec liqueur, ½ oz. of tequila,

½ oz. of gin, ½ oz. of white rum and ½ oz. of vodka
. Top up with cola and stir gently
. Garnish with orange zest

Moscow Mule

prep time: 5 min | technique: build

Ingredients:
2 oz. vodka
5 oz. ginger beer
¼ oz. lime juice
Ice
Lime wedge, for garnish
Mint leaves, for garnish

Gadgets:
cooper mug or rocks glass, jigger, bar spoon, squeezer

Preparation:
. Fill a copper mug to the top with ice
. Pour in ¼ oz. of lime juice
. Pour in 2 oz. of vodka
. Top up with ginger beer and stir gently
. Garnish with a lime wedge and mint leaves

Oldboy

prep time: 5 min | technique: shake

Ingredients:
2 oz. vodka
4 oz. grapefruit juice
Strawberry
Granulated Cane Sugar
Ground cinnamon
Ice
Chili pepper, for garnish

Gadgets:
highball glass, muddler, shaker, strainer, jigger, bar spoon, drinking straws

Preparation:
. Fill a highball glass to the top with ice
. Place 3 strawberries, 2 bar spoons of granulated cane sugar into a shaker and muddle

. Pour 4 oz. of grapefruit juice and 2 oz. of vodka into a shaker
. Fill the shaker with ice cubes and shake
. Strain into the highball glass
. Sprinkle with ground cinnamon and garnish with a chili pepper pod

Salty Dog

prep time: 5 min | technique: build

Ingredients:
2 oz. vodka
6 oz. grapefruit juice
Ice
Salt, for garnish
Grapefruit wedge, for garnish

Gadgets:
rocks glass, jigger, bar spoon, drinking straws

Preparation:
. Rim a rocks glass with salt
. Fill a rocks glass to the top with ice
. Pour in 2 oz. of vodka
. Top up with grapefruit juice and stir gently
. Garnish with a grapefruit wedge

Sea Breeze

prep time: 5 min | technique: build

Ingredients:
2 oz. vodka
2 oz. grapefruit juice
4 oz. cranberry juice
Ice
Cranberry, for garnish
Orange, for garnish

Gadgets:
collins glass, jigger, bar spoon, drinking straws, cocktail skewer

Preparation:
. Fill a collins glass to the top with ice
. Pour in 2 oz. of grapefruit juice and 2 oz. of vodka
. Top up with cranberry juice and stir gently
. Garnish with cranberries and an orange wheel on a cocktail skewer

Sex on the Beach

prep time: 5 min | technique: shake

Ingredients:
2 oz. vodka
1 oz. peach liqueur
1½ oz. cranberry juice
1½ oz. pineapple juice
Ice
Pineapple, for garnish
Raspberry, for garnish

Gadgets:
sling glass, shaker, strainer, jigger, cocktail skewer, drinking straws

Preparation:
. Fill a sling glass to the top with ice
. Pour 1½ oz. of cranberry juice, 1½ oz. of pineapple juice, 1 oz. of peach liqueur and 2 oz. of vodka into a shaker

. Fill the shaker with ice cubes and shake
. Strain into the sling glass
. Garnish with a piece of pineapple and a raspberry on a cocktail skewer

Screwdriver

prep time: 3 min | technique: build

Ingredients:
2 oz. vodka
5 oz. orange juice
Ice
Orange, for garnish

Gadgets:
collins glass, jigger, bar spoon, drinking straws

Preparation:
. Fill a collins glass to the top with ice
. Pour in 2 oz. of vodka
. Top up with orange juice and stir gently
. Garnish with an orange wheel

Vodka Martini

prep time: 3 min | technique: stir

Ingredients:
2½ oz. vodka
½ oz. dry vermouth Martini
Ice
Green olives, for garnish

Gadgets:
cocktail glass, mixing glass, bar spoon, strainer, jigger, cocktail skewer

Preparation:
. Pour ½ oz. of dry vermouth and 2½ oz. of vodka into a mixing glass
. Fill the glass with ice cubes and stir gently
. Strain into a chilled cocktail glass
. Garnish with 3 green olives on a cocktail skewer

White Russian

prep time: 5 min | technique: build

Ingredients:
1 oz. vodka
1 oz. coffee liqueur
1 oz. light cream
Ice

Gadgets:
rocks glass, jigger, bar spoon, drinking straws

Preparation:
. Fill a rocks glass to the top with ice
. Pour in 1 oz. of light cream, 1 oz. of coffee liqueur, 1 oz. of vodka
. Stir until the sides of the glass begin to frost

TEQUILA BASED COCKTAILS

Duke Tulip

prep time: 5 min | technique: shake

Ingredients:
1½ oz. gold tequila
½ oz. vanilla syrup
½ oz. sugar syrup
Lemon
Orange
Raspberry
Rosemary
Ice

Gadgets:
champagne saucer, muddler, jigger, shaker, strainer, sieve

Preparation:
. Place a quarter of lemon, 2 orange wedges, a rosemary sprig into a shaker and muddle

- Pour in ½ oz. of sugar syrup, ½ oz. of vanilla syrup and 1½ oz. of gold tequila
- Fill the shaker with ice cubes and shake
- Finely strain into a chilled champagne saucer
- Garnish with 2 raspberries on a rosemary sprig

Kerman

prep time: 5 min | technique: shake

Ingredients:
1½ oz. silver tequila
¾ oz. pistachio syrup
¾ oz. lime juice
Pink salt
Ice

Gadgets:
cocktail glass, squeezer, jigger, shaker, strainer

Preparation:
. Salt the rim of the glass
. Pour ¾ oz. of lime juice, ¾ oz. of pistachio syrup, and 1½ oz. of silver tequila into a shaker
. Fill the shaker with ice cubes and shake gently
. Strain into a chilled cocktail glass

Margarita

prep time: 5 min | technique: shake

Ingredients:
1½ oz. silver tequila
¾ oz. triple sec liqueur
½ oz. sugar syrup
1 oz. lime juice
Lime
Salt
Ice

Gadgets:
margarita glass, squeezer, jigger, shaker, strainer

Preparation:
. Salt the rim of the glass
. Pour 1 oz. of lime juice, ¾ oz. of triple sec liqueur, ½ oz. of sugar syrup and 1½ oz. of silver tequila into a shaker
. Fill the shaker with ice cubes and shake gently
. Strain into a chilled margarita glass
. Garnish with a lime wheel

Monte Alban

prep time: 5 min | technique: build

Ingredients:
2 oz. silver tequila
½ oz. honey syrup
2 oz. cherry juice
2 oz. pineapple juice
½ oz. lemon juice
Ice
Pineapple, for garnish

Gadgets:
highball glass, squeezer, jigger, bar spoon, cocktail skewer, drinking straws

Preparation:
. Fill a highball glass to the top with ice
. Pour in ½ oz. of lemon juice, ½ oz. of honey syrup, 2 oz. of cherry juice and 2 oz. of silver tequila

. Top up with pineapple juice and stir gently
. Garnish with a small finely chopped pineapple wedge on a cocktail skewer

Old George

prep time: 5 min | technique: shake

Ingredients:
2 oz. silver tequila
1 oz. cucumber syrup
1 oz. lime juice
1 egg white
Green basil leaf
Cardamon
Ice

Gadgets:
sour glass, squeezer, jigger, shaker, strainer

Preparation:
. Pour 1 egg white and 1 oz. of lime juice into a shaker
. Add 1 oz. of cucumber syrup and 2 oz. of silver tequila
. Gently shake without ice

- Fill the shaker with ice cubes and shake one more time
- Strain into the sour glass
- Garnish with a green basil leaf and cardamom

Paloma

prep time: 3 min | technique: build

Ingredients:
2 oz. silver tequila
½ oz. lime juice
5 oz. grapefruit soda
Salt
Lime
Strawberry
Mint
Ice

Gadgets:
highball glass, squeezer, jigger, bar spoon, drinking straws

Preparation:
. Rim a highball glass with salt
. Fill the glass to the top with ice cubes

. Pour in ½ oz. of lime juice and 2 oz. of silver tequila
. Top up with grapefruit soda and stir gently
. Garnish with a chopped strawberry, a lime wheel and a mint sprig

Primavera

prep time: 5 min | technique: stir

Ingredients:
2 oz. silver tequila
½ oz. blueberry jam
Tabasco sauce
Rosemary
Orange zest
Ice

Gadgets:
rocks glass, mixing glass, bar spoon, strainer, jigger, drinking straws, zest knife, sieve

Preparation:
. Fill a rocks glass to the top with ice cubes
. Place 2 bar spoons of blueberry jam and a rosemary sprig into a mixing glass
. Add 3 drops of red Tabasco sauce and 2 oz. of silver tequila

. Fill the mixing glass with ice cubes and stir
. Strain into the rocks glass
. Garnish with a sprig of rosemary and orange zest

Tequila Smash

prep time: 3 min | technique: build

Ingredients:
2 oz. silver tequila
¾ oz. sugar syrup
Lemon
Lime
Mint
Crushed ice

Gadgets:
rocks glass, muddler, jigger, bar spoon, drinking straws

Preparation:
. Place 5 mint leaves and 3 lemon wedges into a rocks glass and muddle
. Fill the rocks glass to the top with crushed ice
. Pour in ¾ oz. of sugar syrup, 2 oz. of silver tequila and stir gently
. Top up with crushed ice
. Garnish with a lime wheel and a mint leaf

Tequila Sunrise

prep time: 3 min | technique: build

Ingredients:
2 oz. silver tequila
½ oz. grenadine syrup
5 oz. orange juice
Orange
Ice

Gadgets:
highball glass, jigger, bar spoon, drinking straws

Preparation:
. Fill a highball glass to the top with ice cubes
. Pour in ½ oz. of grenadine syrup and 2 oz. of silver tequila
. Top up with orange juice and stir gently
. Garnish with an orange wheel

BRANDY BASED COCKTAILS

Brandy Alexander

prep time: 3 min | technique: shake

Ingredients:
1½ oz. cognac
1 oz. dark cacao liqueur
1 oz. light cream
Ice
Ground nutmeg, for garnish

Gadgets:
cocktail glass, jigger, shaker, strainer, nutmeg grater

Preparation:
. Pour 1 oz. of light cream, 1 oz. of dark cacao liqueur and 1½ oz. of cognac into a shaker
. Fill the shaker with ice cubes and shake
. Strain into a chilled cocktail glass
. Garnish with ground nutmeg

Brandy Sour

prep time: 3 min | technique: shake

Ingredients:
2 oz. cognac
1 oz. sugar syrup
¾ oz. lemon juice
1 egg white
Lemon
Maraschino cherry
Ice

Gadgets:
rocks glass, squeezer, jigger, shaker, strainer, cocktail skewer

Preparation:
. Fill a rocks glass to the top with ice cubes
. Pour 1 oz. of quail egg whites, ¾ oz. of lemon juice, 1 oz. of sugar syrup and 2 oz. of cognac into a shaker

. Fill the shaker with ice cubes and shake thoroughly
. Strain into the rocks glass
. Garnish with a lemon wheel and a Maraschino cherry on a cocktail skewer

French Cinnamon

prep time: 3 min | technique: shake

Ingredients:
1 oz. cognac
½ oz. caramel syrup
2 oz. apple juice
Ice
Cinnamon sticks, for garnish

Gadgets:
rocks glass, jigger, shaker, strainer, drinking straws

Preparation:
. Fill a rocks glass to the top with ice cubes
. Pour 2 oz. of apple juice, ½ oz. of caramel syrup and 1 oz. of cognac into a shaker
. Fill the shaker with ice cubes and shake
. Strain into the rocks glass
. Garnish with 2 cinnamon sticks

French Connection

prep time: 3 min | technique: build

Ingredients:
1½ oz. cognac
¾ oz. amaretto liqueur
Ice

Gadgets:
rocks glass, jigger, bar spoon, zest knife

Preparation:
. Fill a rocks glass to the top with ice cubes
. Pour in ¾ oz. of amaretto liqueur and ¾ oz. amaretto liqueur and stir briefly

Horse's Neck

prep time: 3 min | technique: build

Ingredients:
2 oz. cognac
5 oz. ginger ale
Angostura bitters
Lemon zest
Ice

Gadgets:
highball glass, jigger, bar spoon, zest knife

Preparation:
. Fill a highball glass to the top with ice cubes
. Pour in 2 oz. of cognac and 1 dash of Angostura bitters
. Top up with ginger ale and stir gently
. Garnish with long lemon zest

Ruby

prep time: 3 min | technique: shake

Ingredients:
1 oz. cognac
½ oz. apricot liqueur
¼ oz. grenadine syrup
1 oz. orange juice
Ice
Maraschino cherry, for garnish

Gadgets:
cocktail glass, jigger, shaker, strainer, cocktail skewer

Preparation:
. Pour ¼ oz. of grenadine syrup, ½ oz. of apricot liqueur, 1 oz. of orange juice and 1 oz. of cognac into a shaker
. Fill the shaker with ice cubes and shake
. Strain into a chilled cocktail glass
. Garnish with a Maraschino cherry on a cocktail skewer

The Double

prep time: 3 min | technique: shake

Ingredients:
1 ½ oz. cognac
1 oz. grapefruit liqueur
¼ oz. sugar syrup
¾ oz. lemon juice
Ice

Gadgets:
champagne saucer, squeezer, jigger, shaker, strainer

Preparation:
. Pour ¾ oz. of lemon juice, ¼ oz. of sugar syrup, 1 oz. of grapefruit liqueur and 1.5 oz. of cognac into a shaker
. Fill the shaker with ice cubes and shake
. Strain into a chilled champagne saucer

Sidecar

prep time: 3 min | technique: shake

Ingredients:
1½ oz. cognac
1 oz. triple sec liqueur
¼ oz. sugar syrup
¾ oz. lemon juice
½ oz. still water
Ice

Gadgets:
cocktail glass, squeezer, jigger, shaker, strainer

Preparation:
. Pour ¾ oz. of lemon juice, ½ oz. of still water and ¼ oz. of sugar syrup
. Add 1 oz. of triple sec liqueur and 1½ oz. of cognac into a shaker
. Fill the shaker with ice cubes and shake
. Strain into the chilled cocktail glass

Sunset Boulevard

prep time: 5 min | technique: shake

Ingredients:
1 ½ oz. cognac
¾ oz. grenadine syrup
¾ oz. blackcurrant syrup
1 oz. heavy cream
Ice
Maraschino cherry, for garnish

Gadgets:
champagne saucer, jigger, shaker, strainer

Preparation:
. Pour 1 oz. of heavy cream, ¾ oz. of blackcurrant syrup, ¾ oz. of grenadine syrup and 1 ½ oz. of cognac into a shaker
. Fill the shaker with ice cubes and shake thoroughly
. Strain into a chilled champagne saucer
. Garnish with a Maraschino cherry

WHISKY BASED COCKTAILS

Boulevardier

prep time: 3 min | technique: build

Ingredients:
1½ oz. bourbon
1 oz. red vermouth
1 oz. red bitter
Ice
Orange zest, for garnish

Gadgets:
rocks glass, jigger, bar spoon, zest knife

Preparation:
. Fill a rocks glass to the top with ice cubes
. Pour in 1 oz. of red vermouth, 1 oz. of red bitter and 1½ oz. of bourbon
. Stir gently
. Garnish with orange zest

Manhattan

prep time: 5 min | technique: stir

Ingredients:
1½ oz. bourbon
¾ oz. red vermouth
Angostura bitters
Maraschino cherry
Ice

Gadgets:
cocktail glass, mixing glass, bar spoon, strainer, jigger

Preparation:
. Pour ¾ oz. of red vermouth and 1½ oz. of bourbon into a mixing glass
. Add 1 dash of Angostura bitters
. Fill the glass with ice cubes and stir gently
. Strain into a chilled cocktail glass
. Garnish with a Maraschino cherry

Match Point

prep time: 3 min | technique: build

Ingredients:
1½ oz. Irish whiskey
½ oz. lime juice
5 oz. ginger beer
Ice
Lime, for garnish

Gadgets:
goblet glass, squeezer, jigger, bar spoon, drinking straws

Preparation:
. Fill a goblet glass to the top with ice cubes
. Pour in ½ oz. of lime juice and 1½ oz. of Irish whiskey
. Top up with ginger beer and stir gently
. Garnish with a lime wedge

Mint Julep

prep time: 5 min | technique: build

Ingredients:
1½ oz. bourbon
½ oz. still water
Mint
Caster sugar
Crushed ice

Gadgets:
copper mug, muddler, jigger, bar spoon, drinking straws

Preparation:
. Place 10 mint leaves and 2 bar spoons of caster sugar into a copper mug
. Pour in ½ oz. of still water and muddle gently
. Fill the mug to the top with crushed ice
. Pour in 1½ oz. of aged bourbon and stir gently
. Top up with crushed ice
. Garnish with a mint sprig

Old Fashioned

prep time: 3 min | technique: build

Ingredients:
2 oz. bourbon
Angostura bitters
Orange
Cane sugar cubes
Maraschino cherry
Ice

Gadgets:
rocks glass, jigger, muddler, bar spoon

Preparation:
. Place an orange wedge and a red Maraschino cherry into a rocks glass
. Add a cane sugar cube soaked in 1 dash of Angostura bitters and muddle
. Fill the rocks glass with ice cubes
. Pour in 2 oz. of bourbon and stir gently

Rob Roy

prep time: 5 min | technique: stir

Ingredients:
2 oz. Scotch whisky
1½ oz. red vermouth
Angostura bitters
Ice
Orange zest, for garnish

Gadgets:
cocktail glass, mixing glass, bar spoon, strainer, jigger, zest knife, clothespins

Preparation:
. Pour 1½ oz. of red vermouth and 2 oz. of Scotch whisky into a mixing glass
. Add 1 dash of Angostura bitters
. Fill the glass with ice cubes and stir
. Strain into a chilled cocktail glass
. Garnish with orange zest on a clothespin

Rusty Nail

prep time: 3 min | technique: build

Ingredients:
2 oz. Scotch whisky
1 oz. Drambuie
Ice

Gadgets:
rocks glass, jigger, bar spoon

Preparation:
. Fill a rocks glass to the top with ice cubes
. Pour 1 oz. of Drambuie and 2 oz. of Scotch whisky into the rocks glass and stir

The New Yorker

prep time: 3 min | technique: shake

Ingredients:
1 ½ oz. Irish whiskey
¾ oz. grenadine syrup
1 oz. lemon juice
Angostura bitters
Ice
Orange zest, for garnish

Gadgets:
champagne saucer, squeezer, jigger, shaker, strainer, zest knife

Preparation:
. Pour 1 oz. of lemon juice, ¾ oz. of grenadine syrup and 1 ½ oz. of Irish whiskey into a shaker
. Add 2 dashes of Angostura bitters
. Fill the shaker with ice cubes and shake
. Strain into a chilled champagne saucer
. Garnish with orange zest

Whiskey Sour

prep time: 5 min | technique: shake

Ingredients:
1½ oz. bourbon
½ oz. sugar syrup
1 oz. lemon juice
Angostura bitters
Egg white
Lemon
Maraschino cherry
Ice

Gadgets:
rocks glass, squeezer, jigger, shaker, strainer, cocktail skewer

Preparation:
. Fill a rocks glass to the top with ice cubes
. Pour 1 egg white, 1 oz. of lemon juice, ½ oz. of sugar syrup and 1½ oz. of bourbon into a shaker

- Add 1 dash of Angostura bitters and shake
- Fill the shaker with ice cubes and shake again
- Strain into the rocks glass
- Garnish with a lemon wheel and a Maraschino cherry on a cocktail skewer

INDEX

A
Apple Cooler, *17*
Aviation, *39*

B
Beachcomber, *18*
Black Russian, *55*
Bloody Mary, *57*
Blue Hawaiian, *19*
Blue Lagoon, *56*
Boulevardier, *109*
Bramble, *41*
Brandy Alexander, *97*
Brandy Sour, *98*
Bronx, *43*

C
Cable Car, *20*
Caipiroska, *59*
Cape Codder, *60*
Clover Club, *40*
Cosmopolitan, *61*
Cuba Libre, *21*

D
Daiquiri, *22*
Dark'n'Stormy, *23*
Dry Martini, *44*
Duke Tulip, *81*

E
Espresso Martini, *63*

F
French Cinnamon, *100*

French Connection, *101*

G
Gimlet, *45*
Gin and Tonic, *46*

H
Horse's Neck, *102*
Hurricane, *24*

I
IQ, *64*

K
Kamikadze, *65*
Kerman, *83*
Knickerbocker, *26*

L
Long Island Iced Tea, *66*

M
Mai Tai, *27*
Manhattan, *110*
Margarita, *84*
Martinez, *47*
Match Point, *111*
Mint Julep, *112*
Mojito, *29*
Monte Alban, *85*
Moscow Mule, *68*

N
Negroni, *48*

O
Old Fashioned, *113*
Old George, *87*
Oldboy, *69*

P
Painkiller, *31*
Paloma, *89*
Piña Colada, *33*
Planter's Punch, *34*
Primavera, *91*

R
Rob Roy, *114*
Ruby, *103*
Rum Runner, *36*
Rusty Nail, *115*

S
Salty Dog, *71*
Screwdriver, *75*
Sea Breeze, *72*
Sex on the Beach, *73*
Sidecar, *105*
Sunset Boulevard, *106*

T
Tequila Smash, *93*
Tequila Sunrise, *94*
The Double, *104*
The New Yorker, *116*
Tom Collins, *49*

V
Vesper, *51*
Vodka Martini, *76*

W
Whiskey Sour, *117*
White Russian, *77*